GOD Made ME!
HE Made YOU!

ALAN FLORY

God Made Me! He Made You!

Published by Bridgeway Books
P.O. Box 80107
Austin, Texas 78758

For more information about our books, please write to us, call 512.478.2028, or visit our website at www.bridgewaybooks.net.

Printed and bound in China.

Library of Congress Control Number: 2007924467

ISBN-13: 978-1-933538-79-2
ISBN-10: 1-933538-79-1

10 9 8 7 6 5 4 3 2 1

DEDICATION

God Made Me! He Made You! is written for all children and adults who love animals and like to sing. May this book bring the reader a better understanding of God's relationship to all of us, living in His world.

Cows give milk
which makes us strong.
They eat and they chew
all day long.

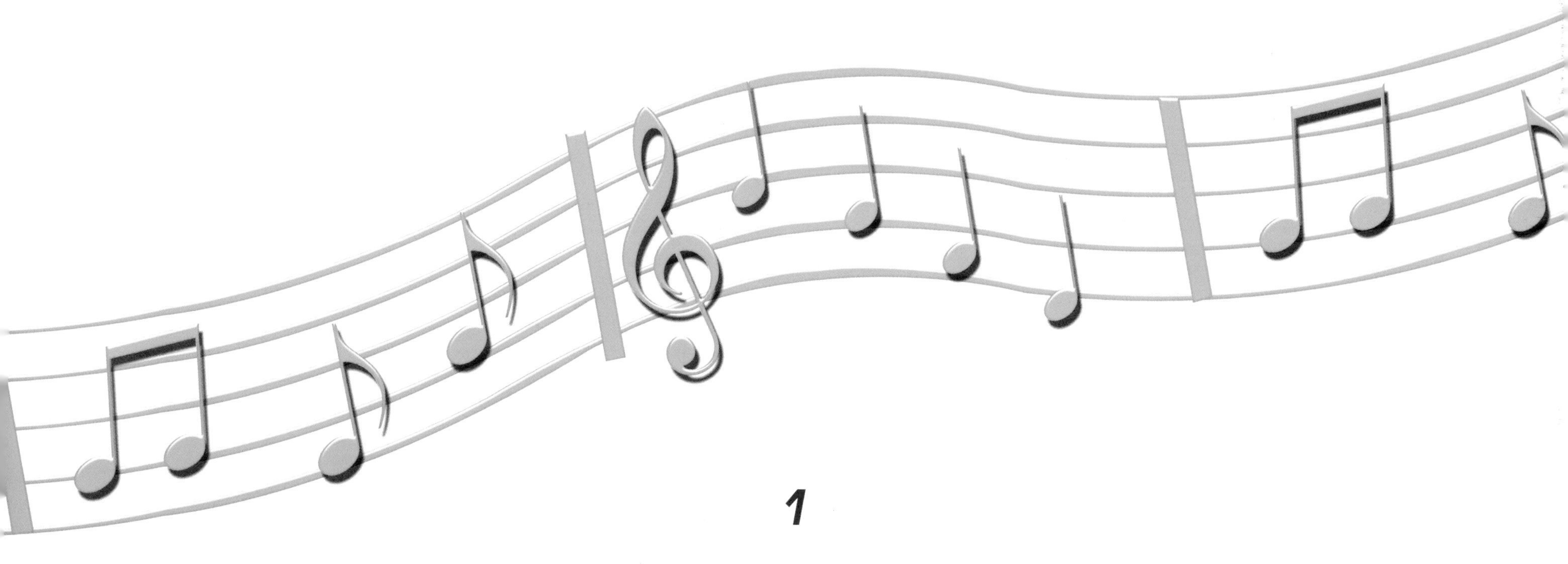

They talk to their friends
in their mooey way.
If you listen real close,
you may hear one say:

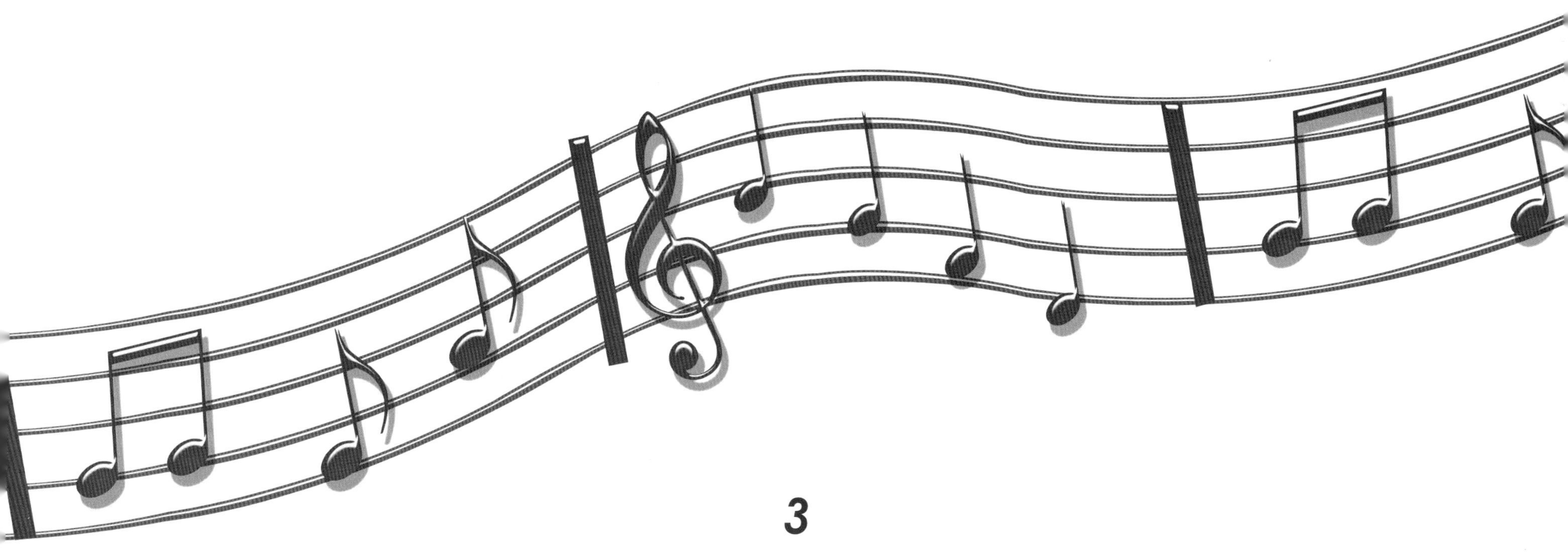

"God made me. He made you. He gave us Jesus; His love is true. Jesus, Jesus, I love You. And, I know You love me too!"

Sheep grow hair.
We call it wool...
which makes warm sweaters
to wear to school.

They talk to their friends
in their sheepy way.
If you listen real close,
you may hear one say:

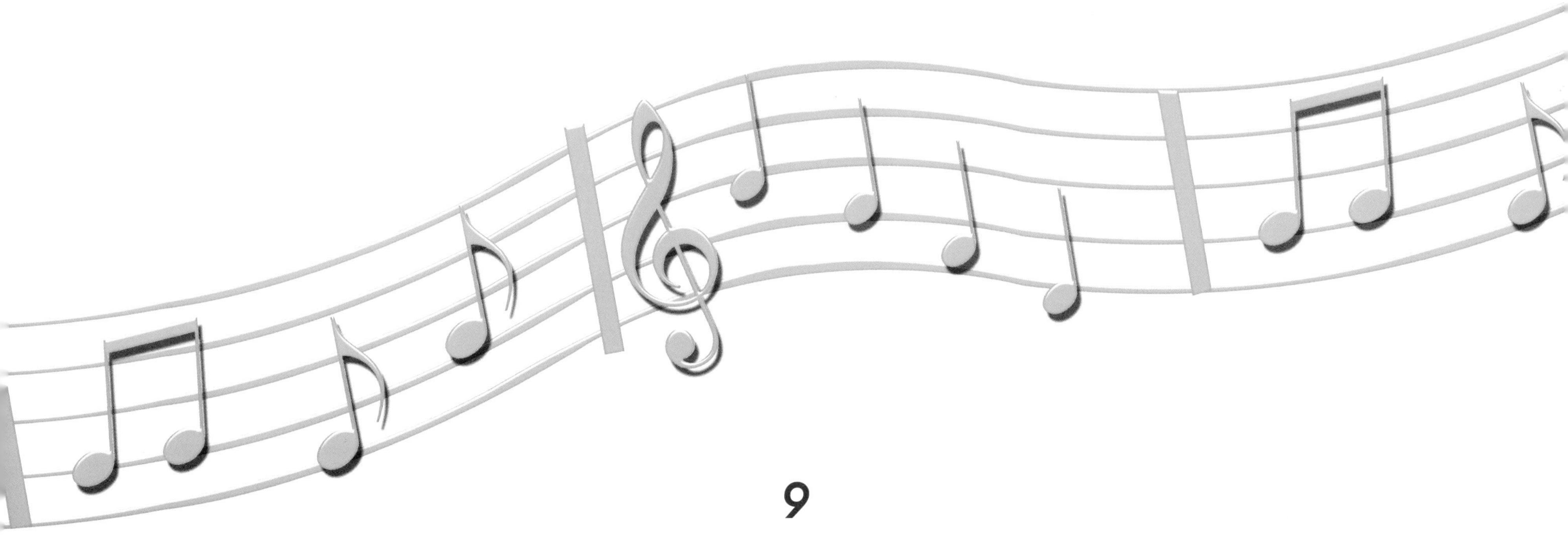

"God made me. He made you. He gave us Jesus; His love is true. Jesus, Jesus, I love You. And, I know You love me too!"

Birds grow feathers
to help them fly.
They build their nests
in the trees...up high!

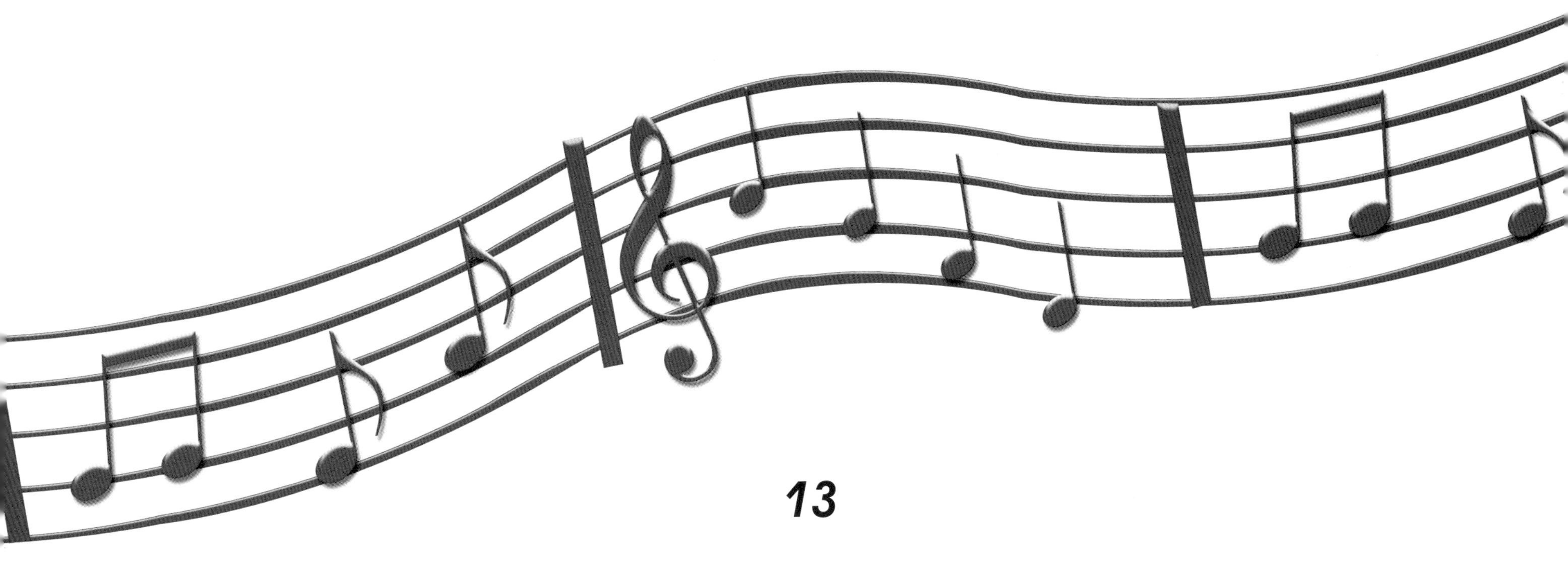

They talk to their friends
in their chirpy way.
If you listen real close,
you may hear one say:

"God made me. He made you. He gave us Jesus; His love is true. Jesus, Jesus, I love You. And, I know You love me too!"

Prairie dogs are curious folk.
They live underground...
that's no joke!

They talk to their friends
in their doggy way.
If you listen real close,
you may hear one say:

"God made me. He made you. He gave us Jesus; His love is true. Jesus, Jesus, I love You. And, I know You love me too!"

Chimpanzees love
to swing in trees.
They even play tag.
They love to tease.

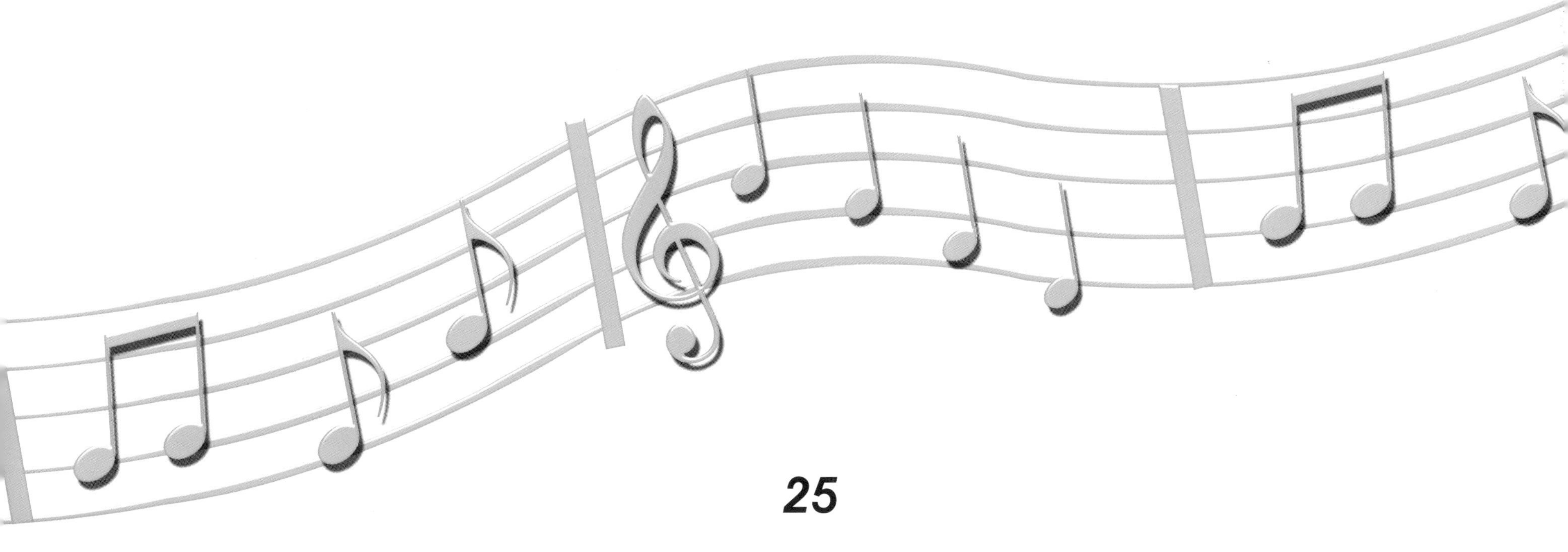

They talk to their friends
in their chimpy way.
If you listen real close,
you may hear one say:

"God made me. He made you. He gave us Jesus; His love is true. Jesus, Jesus, I love You. And, I know You love me too!"

Geese and...

...giraffes understand.

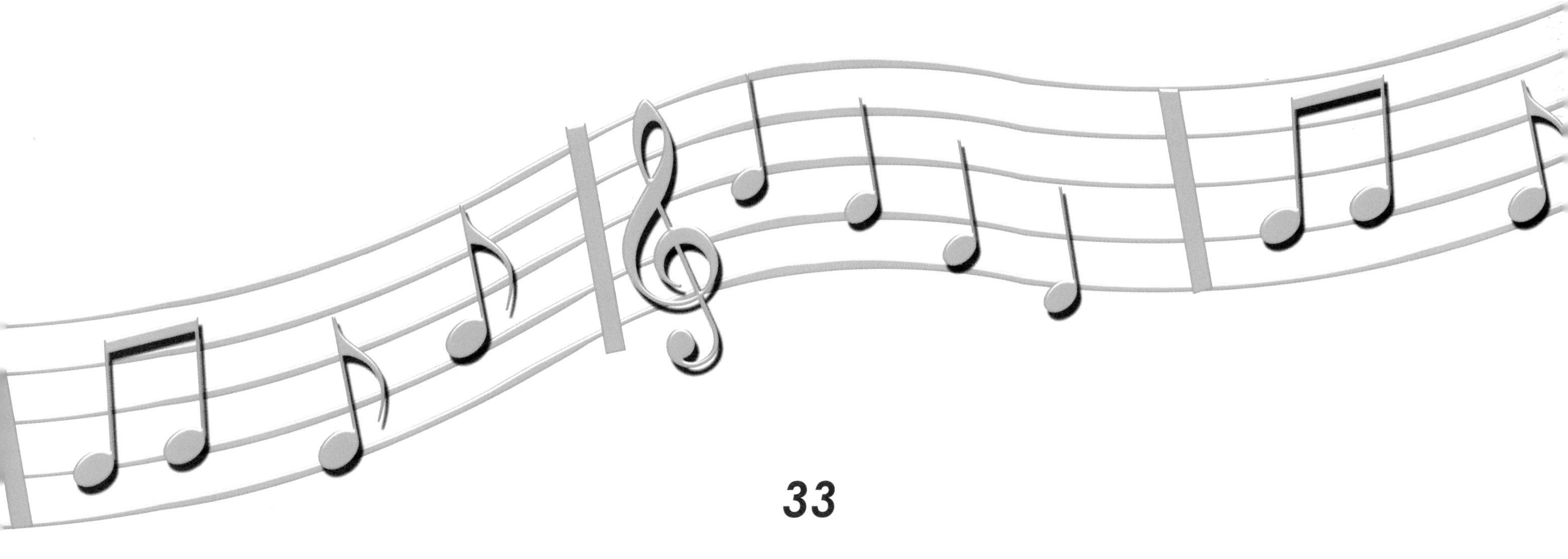

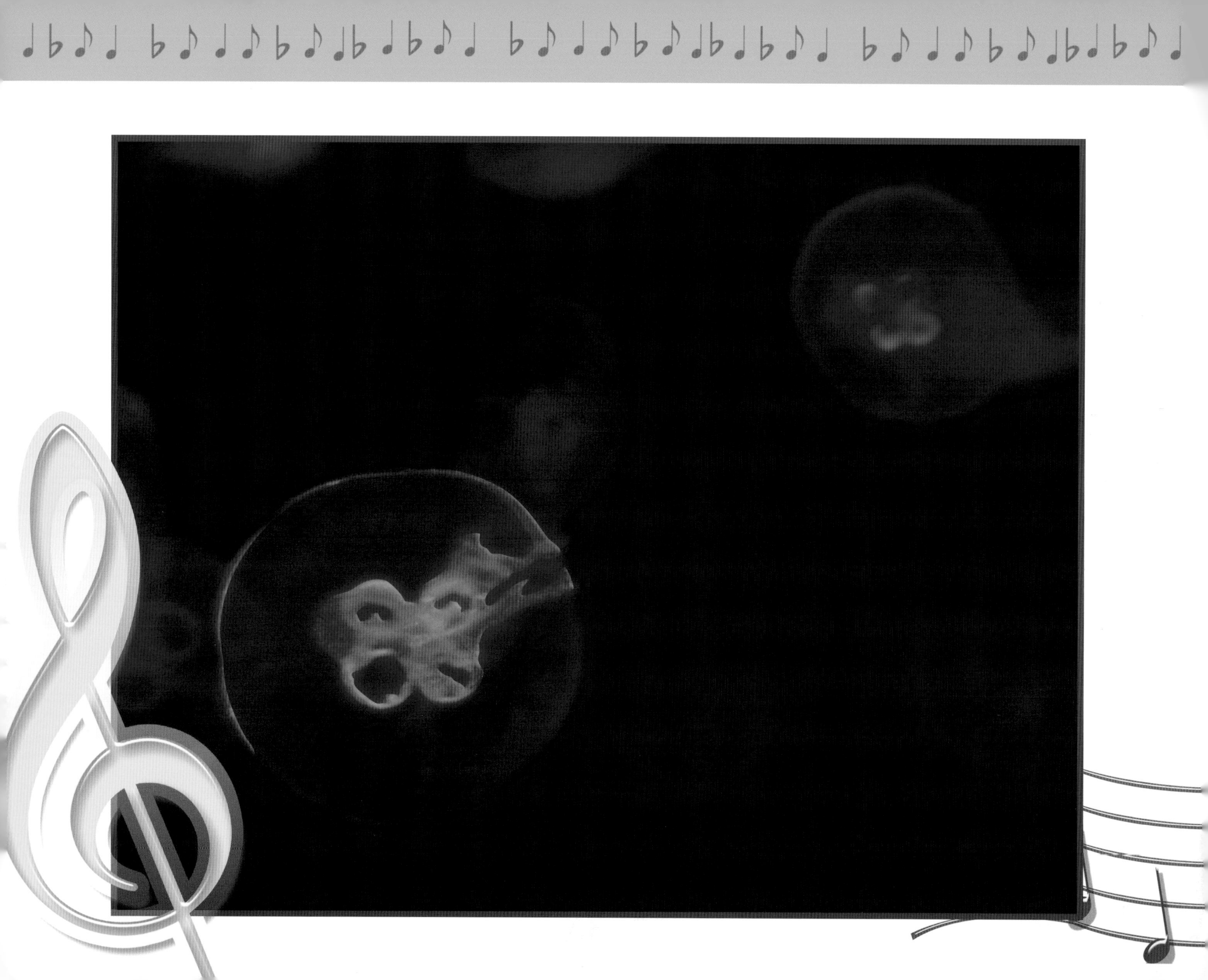

Jellyfish know…

...and so does man!

Each one singing
in harmony...
lifting their voice
in praise to Thee.

They talk to their friends
in their special way.
If you listen real close,
you may hear one say:

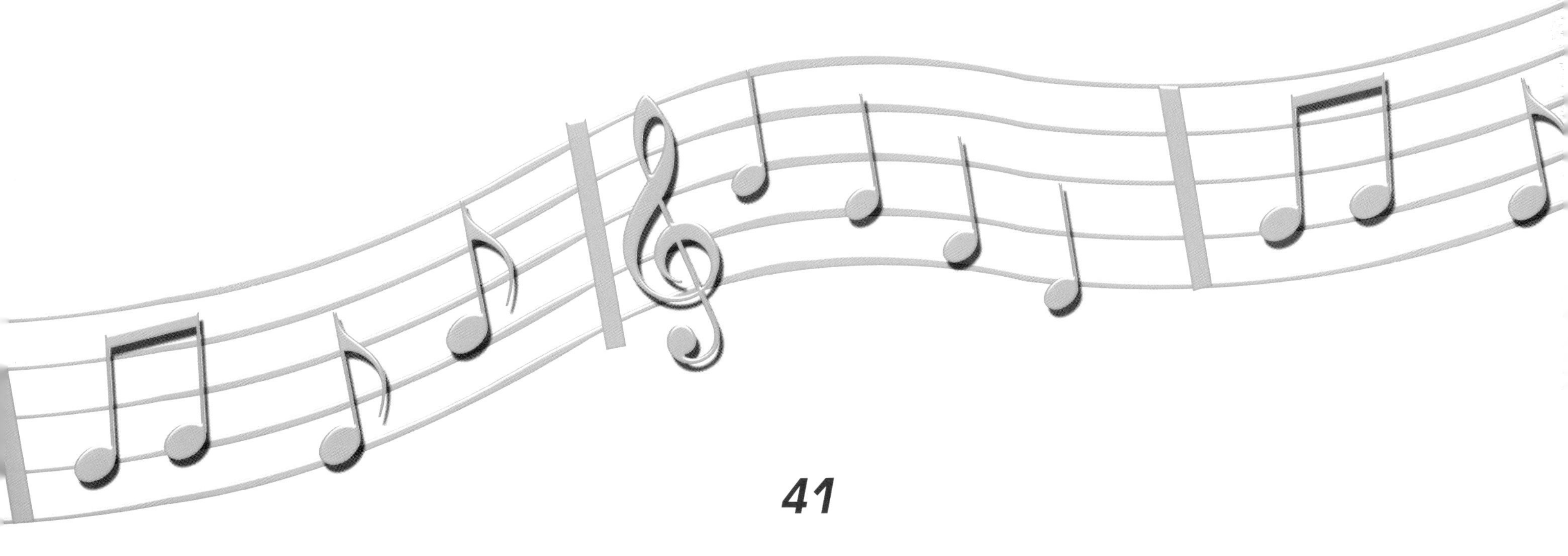

"God made me. He made you. He gave us Jesus; His love is true."

"Jesus, Jesus, I love You. And, I know You love me too!"

It's hard to believe that I have to love a mosquito!
Yeah, but I don't think we want one for a pet!

"God made me. He made you. He gave us Jesus; His love is true. Jesus, Jesus, I love You. And, I know You love me too!"

God Made Me! He Made You!

Words and Music by
Alan L. Flory

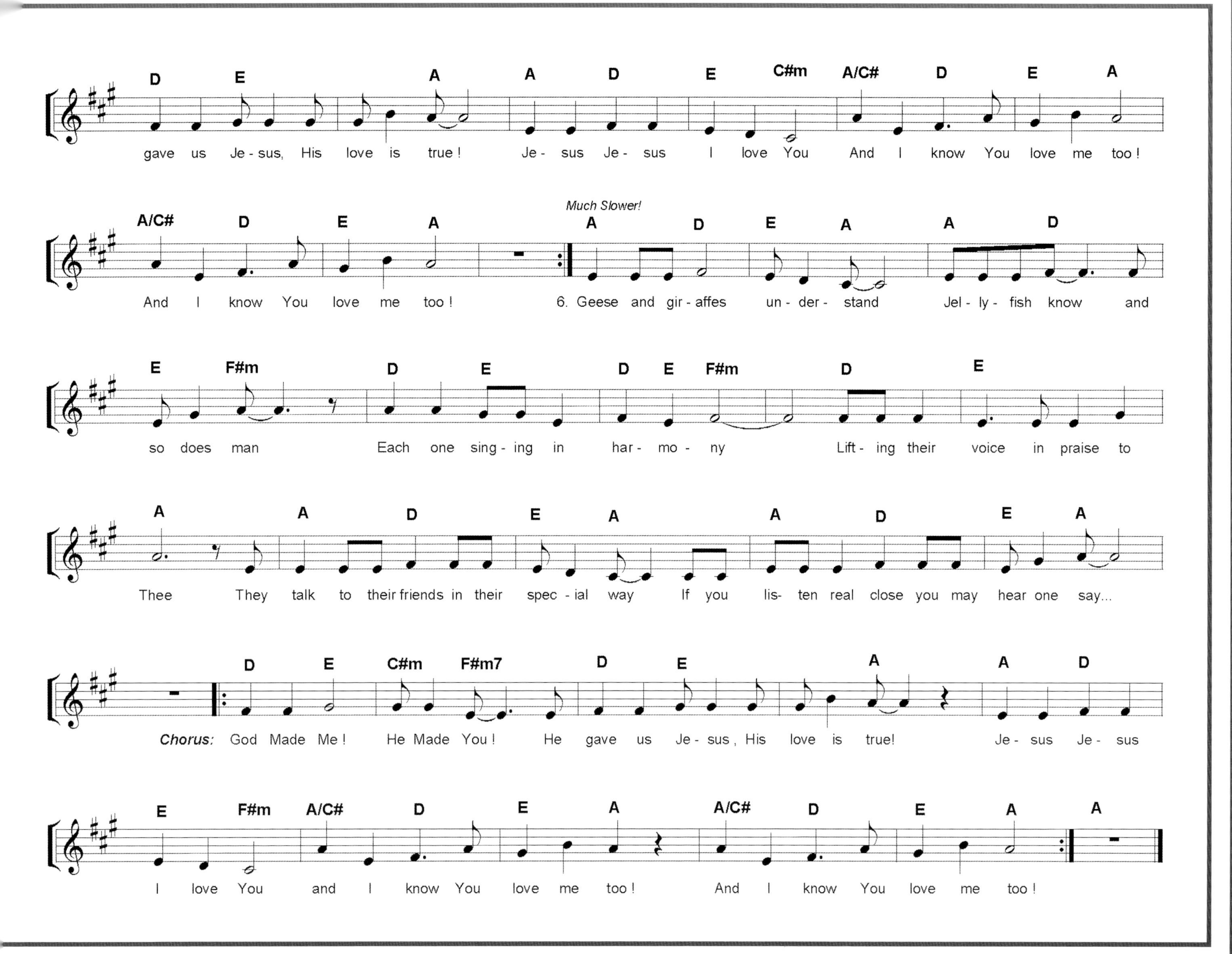
D E A A D E C#m A/C# D E A
gave us Je - sus, His love is true ! Je - sus Je - sus I love You And I know You love me too !
Much Slower!
A/C# D E A A D E A A D
And I know You love me too ! 6. Geese and gir - affes un - der - stand Jel - ly - fish know and
E F#m D E D E F#m D E
so does man Each one sing - ing in har - mo - ny Lift - ing their voice in praise to
A A D E A A D E A
Thee They talk to their friends in their spec - ial way If you lis- ten real close you may hear one say...
D E C#m F#m7 D E A A D
Chorus: God Made Me ! He Made You ! He gave us Je - sus , His love is true! Je - sus Je - sus
E F#m A/C# D E A A/C# D E A A
I love You and I know You love me too ! And I know You love me too !